Morning
Noon and
Nighttime, Too

Morning
Noon and
Nighttime, Too

Poems selected by
Lee Bennett Hopkins

Illustrated by
Nancy Hannans

Harper & Row, Publishers

Morning, Noon and Nighttime, Too
Text copyright © 1980 by Lee Bennett Hopkins
Illustrations copyright © 1980 by Nancy Hannans
All rights reserved. No part of this book may be
used or reproduced in any manner whatsoever without
written permission except in the case of brief quotations
embodied in critical articles and reviews. Printed in
the United States of America. For information address
Harper & Row, Publishers, Inc., 10 East 53rd Street,
New York, N.Y. 10022. Published simultaneously in
Canada by Fitzhenry & Whiteside Limited, Toronto.
First Edition

Library of Congress Cataloging in Publication Data
Main entry under title:
Morning, noon and nighttime, too.
    SUMMARY: An anthology of poems about everyday
activities that takes the reader from breakfast time to
bedtime.
    1. Children's poetry, American. [1. American
poetry—Collections] I. Hopkins, Lee Bennett.
II. Hannans, Nancy.
PS613.M63   811'.008'0355   78-22484
ISBN 0-06-022576-9
ISBN 0-06-022577-7 lib. bdg.

Acknowledgments

Every effort has been made to trace the ownership of all copyrighted material and to secure the necessary permissions to reprint these selections. In the event of any question arising to the use of any material, the editor and the publisher, while expressing regret for any inadvertent error, will be happy to make the necessary correction in future printings. Thanks are due to the following for permission to reprint the copyrighted materials listed below:

Atheneum Publishers, Inc., for "Shadows" by Patricia Hubbell from *Catch Me a Wind* by Patricia Hubbell. Copyright © 1968 by Patricia Hubbell; "History" by Myra Cohn Livingston from *The Way Things Are and Other Poems* by Myra Cohn Livingston (A Margaret K. McElderry Book). Copyright © 1974 by Myra Cohn Livingston; "Dusk" by Myra Cohn Livingston from *4-Way Stop and Other Poems* by Myra Cohn Livingston (A Margaret K. McElderry Book). Copyright © 1976 by Myra Cohn Livingston; "Toaster Time" by Eve Merriam from *There Is No Rhyme for Silver* by Eve Merriam. Copyright © 1962 by Eve Merriam; "Sometimes" and "Walking" by Lilian Moore from *I Feel the Same Way* by Lilian Moore. Copyright © 1967 by Lilian Moore; Judith Thurman for "Zebra" by Judith Thurman from *Flashlight and Other Poems* by Judith Thurman. Copyright © 1976 by Judith Thurman.

Basil Blackwell, Publisher, for "Last Song" by James Guthrie.

Thomas Y. Crowell, Inc., for "Before Breakfast" and "Good Night" by Aileen Fisher from *In One Door and Out the Other: A Book of Poems* by Aileen Fisher. Copyright © 1969 by Aileen Fisher.

Curtis Brown, Ltd., for "Digging for Treasure" and "Some Bird" by Lee Bennett Hopkins from *Charlie's World* by Lee Bennett Hopkins, published by The Bobbs-Merrill Company, Inc. Copyright © 1972 by Lee Bennett Hopkins; "Girls Can, Too!" by Lee Bennett Hopkins. Copyright © 1972 by Lee Bennett Hopkins.

Delacorte Press for an excerpt from *make a circle keep us in* by Arnold Adoff. Copyright © 1975 by Arnold Adoff.

Doubleday and Company, Inc., for an excerpt from "Miss Hortense Rogers, the Grade School Principal" by Mary O'Neill from *People I'd Like to Keep* by Mary O'Neill. Copyright © 1964 by Mary O'Neill.

E. P. Dutton and Company, Inc., for "After Dinner" by Marchette Chute from *Rhymes About Us* by Marchette Chute. Copyright © 1974 by Marchette Chute; "Happy" and "Wiggly Giggles" by Stacy Jo Crossen and Natalie Anne Covell from *Me Is How I Feel* by Stacy Jo Crossen and Natalie Anne Covell. Copyright © 1970 by A. Harris Stone, Stacy Jo Crossen, Natalie Covell, Victoria de Larrea.

Martin Gardner for "Speak Clearly" from *Never Make Fun of a Turtle, My Son* by Martin Gardner. Copyright © 1969 by Martin Gardner.

For Charlotte S. Huck—
spinner of webs
LBH

Morning

Noon and

Nighttime, Too

Zebra

white sun
black
fire escape,

morning
grazing like a zebra
outside my window.

Judith Thurman

Light

Light through white organdy
Bright and mellow,
Right through white organdy
Lightly yellow,
Touching my hand
With a pale warm glow
That started from
A burning sun
Millions of miles ago.

Felice Holman

Morning

Everyone is tight asleep,
I think I'll sing a tune,
And if I sing it loud enough
I'll wake up someone—soon!

Myra Cohn Livingston

Making Beds

It's the mornings that I dread
When I get up out of bed
And survey the sheets in clumps
Showing off the mattress lumps
That destroyed my sleep last night
When the blankets were too tight
And I threw them on the floor
Letting out a fiendish roar.

After such an awful night
How can I stand up and fight
Flapping sheets and giant mattress
(Everything gets worse with practice)
In the morning I'm so hazy
Making beds can drive me crazy.

Steven Kroll

See, I Can Do It

See, I can do it all myself
With my own little brush!
The tooth paste foams inside my mouth.
The faucet waters rush.

In and out and underneath
And round and round and round:
First I do my upstairs teeth
And then I do my down—

The part I like the best of it
Is at the end, though, when I spit.

Dorothy Aldis

Before Breakfast

Mother has to comb her hair,
Father has to shave,
but I keep getting hungry
with the time I save.

Aileen Fisher

The Toaster

A silver-scaled Dragon with jaws flaming red
Sits at my elbow and toasts my bread.
I hand him fat slices, and then, one by one,
He hands them back when he sees they are done.

William Jay Smith

from Egg Thoughts
Soft-Boiled

I do not like the way you slide,
I do not like your soft inside,
I do not like you many ways,
And I could do for many days
Without a soft-boiled egg.

Russell Hoban

Digging for Treasure

I put my hand in
and found—

    a rusty skate key,
    a part of a tool,
    a dead bee I was saving
    to take into school;

    my library card
    and
    a small model rocket.

I guess it is time
to clean out
my pocket.

        Lee Bennett Hopkins

Things that Happen

Only a while ago,
I saw a snail
running
down the road,
a worm
hopping,
and heard
a toad
singing
like a bird.

The sun rises!
The sun rises!
Can there be
Still more surprises?

Felice Holman

Day-Time Moon

In the morning when the sun
Is shining down on everyone
How strange to see a daytime moon
Floating like a pale balloon
Over house and barn and tree
Without one star for company.

Dorothy Aldis

Shadows

Chunks of night
Melt
In the morning sun.
One lonely one
Grows legs
And follows me
To school.

Patricia Hubbell

Going To School

Going to school
I pass a street
where there is a hardware store
and next to it
a flower shop.

I like to stop
and greet
the flowers on display,
then see next door
different kinds of blooms:
bright paint cans,
shiny pots and pans,
a bouquet
of mops and brooms.

Eve Merriam

Yawning

Sometimes—I'm sorry—but sometimes,
Sometimes, yes, sometimes I'm bored.
It may be because I'm an idiot;
It may be because I'm floored;

It may be because it is raining,
It may be because it is hot,
It may be because I have eaten
Too much, or because I have not.

But sometimes I *cannot* help yawning
(I'm sorry!) the whole morning through—
And when Teacher's turning her back on us,
It may be that she's yawning too.

Eleanor Farjeon

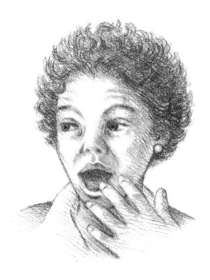

If kids could be the teachers,
If kids could make the rules,
There'd be a lot of changes made
In almost all the schools.
First thing they'd stop the homework.
They'd never give a test.
They know that growing children
Must have their proper rest.
They'd make the lunchtime longer—
Let's say from twelve to two,
So every growing boy or girl
Had time enough to chew!

Bobbi Katz

Wiggly Giggles

I've got the wiggly-wiggles today,
And I just can't sit still.
My teacher says she'll have to find
A stop-me-wiggle pill.

I've got the giggly-giggles today;
I couldn't tell you why.
But if Mary hiccups one more time
I'll giggle till I cry.

I've got to stamp my wiggles out
And hold my giggles in,
Cause wiggling makes me giggle
And gigglers never win.

Stacy Jo Crossen
and Natalie Anne Covell

I'm fixing a lunch for a dinosaur.
Who knows when one might come by?
I'm pulling up all the weeds I can find.
I'm piling them high as the sky.
I'm fixing a lunch for a dinosaur.
I hope he will stop by soon.
Maybe he'll just walk down my street
and have some lunch at noon.

Bobbi Katz

Toaster Time

Tick tick tick tick tick tick tick
Toast up a sandwich quick quick quick
Hamwich
Jamwich
Lick lick lick!

Tick tick tick tick tick tick—stop!
   POP!

Eve Merriam

from If I Were A . . .

If I were a sandwich,
I'd sit on a plate
And think of my middle
Until someone ate
Me.
End of the sandwich.

Karla Kuskin

Happy Marbles!

A girl had one marble.
A boy came and played with her and he won.
Then she had no marbles.
There were plenty of marbles to buy
but the girl had no money to buy.
But the girl had a friend.
And the friend came and gave her a marble.
And then, the boy who had won away her first marble
came again and gave it back to her.
Now the girl has two marbles. She is VERY HAPPY.
She sings this song.
Happy marbles
Happy marbles
Happy marbles
to all—
Happy marbles
Happy marbles
Happy marbles
Hooray! to ALL

Ruth Krauss

Sometimes

Sometimes
when I skip or hop
or when I'm
      jumping

Suddenly
I like to stop
and listen to me
      thumping.

Lilian Moore

from Miss Hortense Rogers, the Grade School Principal

"Why did you pinch
Little Johnny Carew?
He's never been known
To bother you.
And you stuck out your tongue
At your teacher, too.
Why did you grab
Emmy Rimini's ball,
And trip her coming
Down the hall? . . .
Is it because young
Johnny Carew
Doesn't walk home from school
With you?
It couldn't be *that*—
Or could it be?
How old was I when
That happened to me?"
I think she was thumbing
Through her mind
For something lost that
She had to find,
Because for a while
She stood real still

With her hands on the edge
Of the window sill
And when she turned
I could sort of see
The third-grade girl
She used to be,
With bright red hair
And hoppity feet
Running down a
Village street
Smelling things that
Teased her nose
In the time of the
Butterfly
And the rose. . . .

Mary O'Neill

History

And I'm thinking how to get out
Of this stuffy room
With its big blackboards.

And I'm trying not to listen
In this boring room
To the way things *were*.

And I'm thinking about later,
Running from the room
Back into the world,

And what the guys will say when
I'm up to bat and hit
A big fat home run.

Myra Cohn Livingston

Girls Can, Too!

Tony said: "Boys are better!
        They can . . .

        whack a ball,
        ride a bike with one hand
        leap off a wall."

I just listened
        and when he was through,
I laughed and said:
        "Oh, yeah! Well girls can, too!"

Then I leaped off the wall,
        and rode away
With *his* 200 baseball cards
        I *won* that day.

Lee Bennett Hopkins

Space Swing

When my swing goes up to the sky of blue,
I can touch the sun with the tip of my shoe.
Away up high where the white clouds race,
I play I'm an astronaut out in space.
I guess that a moon trip might be fun,
But here in my swing I can touch the sun.

Margaret Hillert

Farther Than Far

I look into the sky and see
The leafy branches of a tree,
And higher still a bird in flight,
And higher still a cloud of white.
Beyond the cloud is lots more sky,
Farther than far, higher than high.
And where it ends, another place
Is filled with space and space and space.

Margaret Hillert

This Is My Rock

This is my rock,
And here I run
To steal the secret of the sun;

This is my rock,
And here come I
Before the night has swept the sky;

This is my rock,
This is the place
I meet the evening face to face.

David McCord

Dinnertime

It's time to come indoors,
To leave
    the sidewalks and the grass;
    to shake the sand, to put away
    our balls, our skates—the games we play;
    to close the back door on the day.
It's time to come indoors.

Myra Cohn Livingston

Some Bird

The sparrow
flew down
to the sidewalk
to stop my game of handball.

I wonder
if he heard my mother calling
me to supper for the
third time?

Lee Bennett Hopkins

from *The People, Yes*

"What's the matter up there?"
"Playing soldier."
"But soldiers don't make that kind of noise."
"We're playing the kind of soldier that
  makes that kind of noise."

Carl Sandburg

Happy

When my daddy comes home
And wants to see
Just me,
I'm happy!
When we find his special chair
And he smooths my messy hair,
I'm happy!
Sometimes he tells me silly stories
Or says funny words over and over
And then tickles me.
We sing songs, make oogly faces
Or he chases me real fast.
When my daddy comes right home
And wants to see
Just me,
I'm happy!

Stacy Jo Crossen
and Natalie Anne Covell

Turtle Soup

Beautiful Soup, so rich and green,
Waiting in a hot tureen !
Who for such dainties would not stoop ?
Soup of the evening, beautiful Soup !
Soup of the evening, beautiful Soup !
    Beau—ootiful Soo—oop !
    Beau—ootiful Soo—oop !
Soo—oop of the e—e—evening,
    Beautiful, beautiful Soup !

Beautiful Soup ! Who cares for fish,
Game, or any other dish ?
Who would not give all else for two p
ennyworth only of beautiful Soup ?
Pennyworth only of beautiful Soup ?
    Beau—ootiful Soo—oop !
    Beau—ootiful Soo—oop !
Soo—oop of the e—e—evening,
    Beautiful, beauti—FUL SOUP !

Lewis Carroll

Speak Clearly

You're old enough to know, my son,
    It's really awfully rude
If someone speaks when both his cheeks
    Are jammed and crammed with food.

Your mother asked you how you liked
    The onions in the stew.
You stuffed your mouth with raisin bread
    And mumbled, "Vewee goo."

Then when she asked you what you said,
    You took a drink of milk,
And all that we could understand
    Was, "Uggle gluggle skwilk."

And now you're asking me if you
    Can have more lemon jello.
Please listen carefully. "Yes, ifoo
    Arstilla ungwy fello."

Martin Gardner

After Dinner

When it is evening
  And dinner is through
This is what
  We would like to do:
Go in the garden
  Where we can run
And finish the games
  We have begun,
With nobody calling,
  "Come in soon,"
Nobody calling
  Under the moon.

Marchette Chute

Dusk

Peeking from her room,
Parting thin white cloud curtains,
Lady Moon smiles.

Myra Cohn Livingston

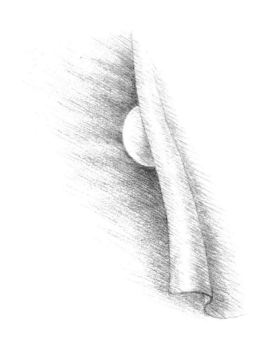

Walking

I stop—
     it stops, too.
It goes when I do.

Over my shoulder I can see
The moon is taking a walk with me.

Lilian Moore

Lullaby

The trees now look scary.
It's dusk and we're wary
       of hedges and sedges
       that border the edges
       of birches and larches,
       and beeches in arches,
       of maples and apples
       and shadows in dapples.
The willows are weeping.
It's time we were sleeping.

Felice Holman

Wordless words.
A tuneless tune.
Blow out the sun.
Draw down the shade.
Turn off the dog.
Snap on the stars.
Unwrap the moon.
Wish leafy, sleeping trees good night
And listen
To the day shut tight.

Karla Kuskin

night

up

    to bed   your head
    down on the pillow

up

    to chin   your covers
    warm and tight   tuck in

                    tuck in
                    tuck in

    kiss
    me
    good

        Arnold Adoff

Good Night

This day's done.
Tomorrow's another.

Good night, Daddy.
Good night, Mother.

Good night, kitten,
book, and brother . . .

In one dream
and out the other.

Aileen Fisher

The Night

As I curl up to go to sleep
I have such lovely thoughts
The darkness of my room,
The warmness of my bed
And what the day has brought.

Amy Goodman

I Never Hear

I never hear my mother come
Into my room late late at night.
She says she has to look and see
If I'm still tucked exactly right.
Nor do I feel her kissing me.
She says she does, though,
Every night.

Dorothy Aldis

Last Song

To the Sun
Who has shone
   All day,
To the Moon
Who has gone
   Away,
To the milk-white,
Silk-white,
Lily-white Star
A fond goodnight
Wherever you are.

James Guthrie

Index of Authors and Titles

Designed by Kohar Alexanian
Set in 12 pt. Century Schoolbook
Composed by Royal Composing Room
Printed by The Murray Printing Company
Bound by The Book Press
HARPER & ROW, PUBLISHERS, INCORPORATED